John Thompson's Modern Course for the Piano

The FIRST GRADE BOOK
Something New Every Lesson

Verses by
Katherine Faith

Drawings by
Frederick S. Manning

A CLEAR, CORRECT AND COMPLETE FOUNDATION IN THE STUDY OF THE PIANO TO ENABLE THE PUPIL TO THINK AND FEEL MUSICALLY

THE WILLIS MUSIC COMPANY

Order No: WMR000022

PREFACE

THIS book is designed for the use of FIRST GRADE pupils. Perhaps the greatest recommendation is that it 'makes haste slowly'. Many bad habits which hamper students in the upper grades are to be traced directly to faulty training in the **beginning.** Thus, many hours of labour, and much financial outlay is incurred annually in the sometimes hopeless task of attempting to correct attitudes, habits and mistakes that should never have been allowed to take root in the first place. "As the twig is bent, the tree's inclined"; this old aphorism applies equally to MUSCULAR CONTROL, TECHNIQUE, TIME PROBLEMS, MUSICAL CONCEPTION, HABITS OF THOUGHT and PRACTICE.

MAKE A SHOWING WITH PUPILS

It is reasonable to assume that most errors are due, less to inattention on the part of the teacher than to an eagerness to SEE THE PUPIL PROGRESS RAPIDLY. Sometimes they may be the fruit of using *wrong material.* A great many early grade books have been apparently written for the exclusive use of "budding geniuses," of whom there are all too few. Yet, even these would benefit immeasurably from a sounder method of learning fundamentals which, in a final analysis, have to be mastered anyway in the end at a great sacrifice of time and energy. The pupil who *thoroughly masters* every simple step as it presents itself, and learns to play his little compositions *cleanly, correctly and UP TO SPEED* will make a far better showing than the one who is allowed to stumble in desultory fashion through more pretentious music.

THIS IS A FIRST GRADE BOOK

This is a *first grade book* which is written in the five-finger position throughout, but in which a few examples of *one finger extension* have been included towards the end. It is for any pupil of average age, and it is assumed that such pupil has had some preliminary piano work in a preparatory grade book.

OBJECTIVES

The purpose of this book is to lay a clear, correct and complete foundation for piano study, to enable the pupil to THINK and FEEL musically. It is quite possible to teach pupils of the first grade how to play with musical understanding. Though they play simple melodies and very modest little pianistic patterns, they should be impressed with the fact that these are the bricks, as it were, which, when laid together, build the greatest compositions. If they learn to recognize and perform these small fragments properly and with intelligence they will meet the larger forms of composition as they progress with perfect understanding, and will not be bewildered at the weaving together of many musical fragments to form a perfect whole.

THE IMPORTANCE OF PATTERNS

With this in mind, the author lays much stress in this book on MELODY PATTERNS, RHYTHMICAL PATTERNS, HARMONY PATTERNS and FINGER PATTERNS. Any elementary pupil who learns to recognize patterns is a better Sight Reader, Memorizer, Interpreter and, through a knowledge of finger patterns, a better pianist than the child who laboriously learns his compositions *note by note.* A note by note conception of music is not only *antiquated* but apt to lessen interest and retard progress. Do not allow students to acquire this conception if **you** wish to keep them interested.

Preface (*Contd.*)

FIVE-FINGER POSITONS

Practically all of the examples in this book remain in the FIVE FINGER POSITION. For this reason TRANSPOSITION IS QUITE EASY by means of *finger patterns*, and the pupil is given opportunity through ACTUAL EXPERIENCE to develop a real finger sense in five-finger groups before venturing into more complicated fingering. The five-finger group is the basis for scale and arpeggio fingering which follow later. Scales and Arpeggi of course, are the foundation of all piano technique: Therefore five-finger drills should not be passed over in a superficial manner.

VARIATIONS ON FIVE-FINGER GROUPS

As pupils become familiar with several five-finger positions (C major, F major, G major, etc.) they are, IN THIS BOOK, gradually introduced to examples combining more than one five-finger group. In other words, they learn that it is no more difficult to change from one five-finger position to another *in the same piece* than it is to do so in two pieces—each one of which requires a different position.

Pupils are also taught to recognize five-finger groups *with extensions*, that is, with one note added on either side of the group.

These simple extensions can be played without shifting the hands out of position. Such extensions also make it possible to enrich both the melodic and harmonic content of the little examples which, ordinarily grow very monotonous when kept strictly within the five-note limit for the entire content of a book.

KEYBOARD ATTACKS

Since the piano is, after all a mechanical instrument made up of keys, strings, hammers and other mundane materials, all our thoughts and emotions must be produced through it by the mechanical action of these mediums in direct communcation with our fingers. The proper TOUCH must be acquired or, regardless of the emotions of the performer, the piano will not respond. Therefore, THE SAME KEYBOARD ATTACKS USED BY THE GREAT ARTISTS SHOULD BE TAUGHT IN MINIATURE TO THE BEGINNER.

Resolve that your pupils are to have the benefit of such training *now*. In perusing this book you will find that the following touches are definitely stressed:—*Finger Legato, Phrasing Attack, Wrist staccato, Forearm Legato and Staccato.* If properly and carefully applied they will enable the beginner to play little pieces with precision, expression and musical understanding. When he has finished the book, the pupil will be ready and eager for his next step up the musical ladder into GRADE TWO. He has learned, to play his piano as a musical instrument and not as a sort of typewriter.

John Thompson

P. S. Certificates of Merit have been included on page 79 as awards for "Examination Reviews" pages 20, 39, 57 and 75.—J. T.

4

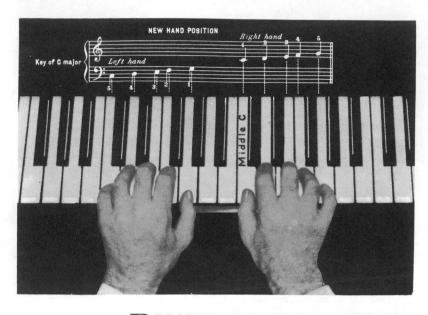

BEFORE beginning to play this piece, PLACE THE HANDS IN THE POSITION shown above. Play each hand separately a few times to get the FEEL of the five finger position in the key of C MAJOR.

1. MUSIC LAND

1st Phrase

Off I go to mu - sic land,

2nd Phrase

Train - ing ear and eye and hand.

THE PHRASE

Music is a language. It can express thoughts and even tell stories—*musical stories.* When we hear a story we listen *sentence by sentence*, NOT letter by letter. So it is with music. Single notes by themselves mean nothing. Only when the notes are arranged into musical sentences do they take on a definite meaning. Musical sentences are called PHRASES. **Learn** to think of your music *phrase by phrase.* Note how the little musical story above **is told in** TWO PHRASES.

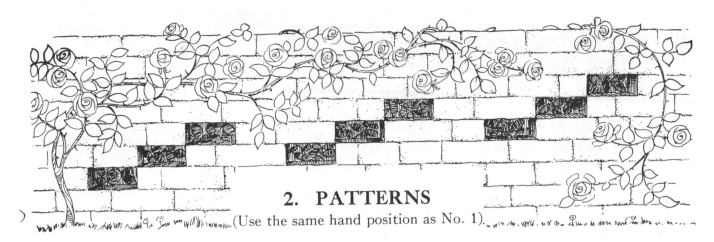

2. PATTERNS

(Use the same hand position as No. 1).

1st Phrase

Build-ers make their hous-es from a pat-tern that is neat.

2nd Phrase

Mu-sic has its pat-terns too with place for *phrase* and *beat.*

MUSICAL FORM

Because it is built up of many well ordered PATTERNS, music has often been compared to architecture. We have in music, *Melody Patterns*, *Rhythmical Patterns*, *Harmony Patterns* and (in piano music) *Finger Patterns*. The ability to recognize PATTERNS is very important. It makes for easier Sight-Reading, quicker Memorizing and more intelligent Interpretation.

THE MELODY PATTERN

The same PATTERN one white key higher.

The same PATTERN another white key higher.

Fix in your mind the above melody pattern in the right hand and note **that** the notes move THREE STEPS upward and ONE SKIP downward.

Note now that this design is repeated over and over throughout the little composition. Each design starting ONE NOTE higher than the preceding pattern.

Melody Pattern | One white key higher | Another white key higher

Practise C major hand position as in No. 1.

THE TIE

The TIE is a curved line joining one note to another of the SAME PITCH and means that the second note is to be held for its full value *without being struck*.

3. RUN-AWAY RIVER

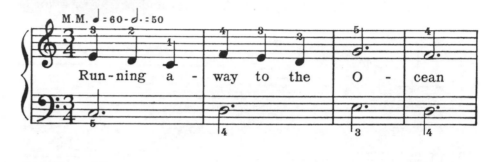

Run-ning a - way to the O - cean

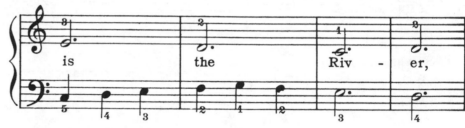

is the Riv - er,

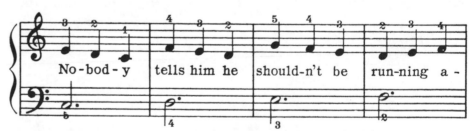

No-bod-y tells him he should-n't be run-ning a-

way at all.

RHYTHM and ACCENTS

RHYTHM has been called the *Soul of Music*. Rhythmical "swing" gives life to any composition. The first step in setting the RHYTHM is by means of the ACCENT. An ACCENT is a special emphasis placed upon ONE of the beats in a bar. RUN-AWAY RIVER is written in THREE-FOUR rhythm, which means ONE count to each crotchet and THREE counts to each bar. *Always accent the first beat of each bar in three-four rhythm.*

COUNT: | **ONE** two three | **ONE** two three | etc.

TWO-FOUR rhythm means ONE count to each crotchet and TWO counts to each bar. *Accent the FIRST note of each bar.*

COUNT: | **ONE** two | **ONE** two | etc.   Use the C major hand position.

Hunt for the MELODY PATTERNS
Think of your pieces PHRASE by PHRASE.

4. THE TRAFFIC COP

TEMPO

TEMPO means TIME. A steady, even TEMPO is necessary to preserve the rhythmical swing. This means that there is no time to stop and hunt for notes or fingers. After a piece has been learned it should be reviewed until it can be played fluently and easily without stops or hesitation.

TONAL SHADING:—As a painter creates beautiful pictures by lights and shadows so in music do we add colour to our musical pictures by means of TONAL SHADING. A MELODY LINE should constantly change in "thickness." This may be accomplished by adding MORE or LESS *intensity* to the tone. Everything possible should be done to make our music "flow." This applies equally to *Melody, Rhythm and Harmony.* "Contrast is the first Law of all Art."

5. SWANS ON THE LAKE

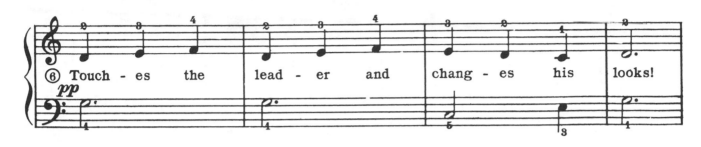

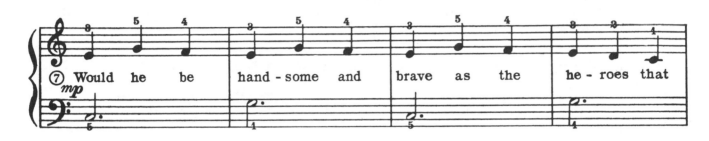

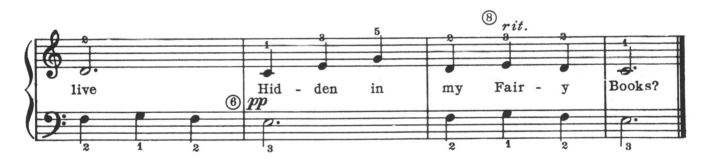

THE MEANING OF THE EXPRESSION MARKS USED IN THIS PIECE

—Read Carefully—

(1) **MODERATO**—*At a moderate rate of speed or tempo.*
(2) **LEGATO**—*Bound together, play smoothly and connected.*
(3) *mf* = Mezzo-forte. *Half or moderately loud.*
(4) *p* = Piano. *Softly.*
(5) *f* = Forte. *Loud.*
(6) *pp* = Pianissimo *Very soft.*
(7) *mp* = Mezzo-piano. *Half or moderately soft.*
(8) **Rit.** = Ritardando. *Gradual slowing up of tempo.*

SEMITONES
(Half Steps)
A SEMITONE is the distance between any Key and the NEXT nearest Key to it.

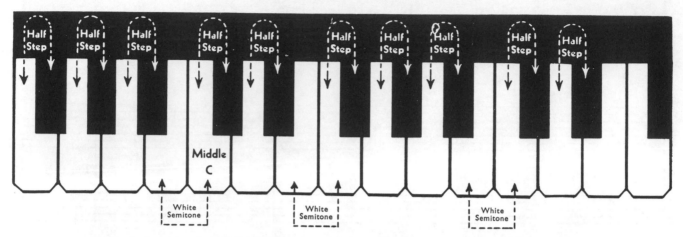

We find most of the SEMITONES are from a WHITE to a BLACK Key. There are, however, two WHITE SEMITONES—one between B and C and the other between E and F. Study them on this chart and locate them on the keyboard of your piano until they can be quickly recognized.

♯ ♯ ♯ ♯ SHARPS AND FLATS ♭ ♭ ♭ ♭

A SHARP (♯) placed before a note RAISES it a SEMITONE
(Half Step)

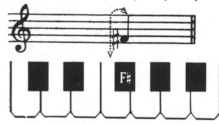

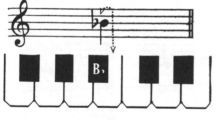

A FLAT (♭) placed before a note LOWERS it a SEMITONE
(Half Step)

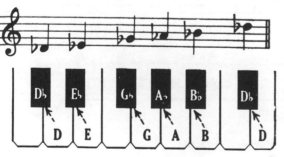

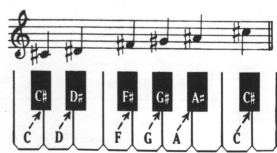

Always **B**e **C**areful to remember that

*A **BLACK** Key to the left of a white key is a FLAT (♭). A **BLACK** to the right of a white key is a SHARP (♯).*

♮ ♮ ♮ NATURAL ♮ ♮ ♮

A NATURAL (♮) placed before a note which has been either SHARPED or FLATTED cancels the SHARP or FLAT.

WHOLE TONES
(Whole Steps)

A WHOLE TONE is twice the distance of a semitone. Therefore, there will always be ONE KEY—either BLACK or WHITE lying between.

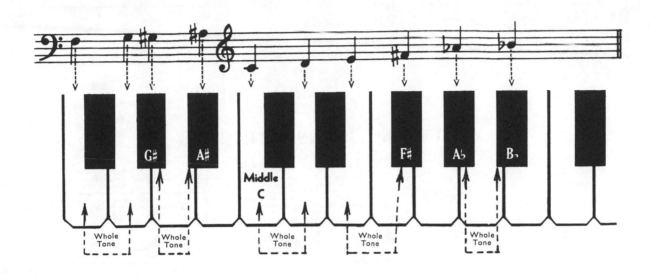

WHOLE TONES AND SEMITONES

Describe the following examples in terms of whole tones and semitones.

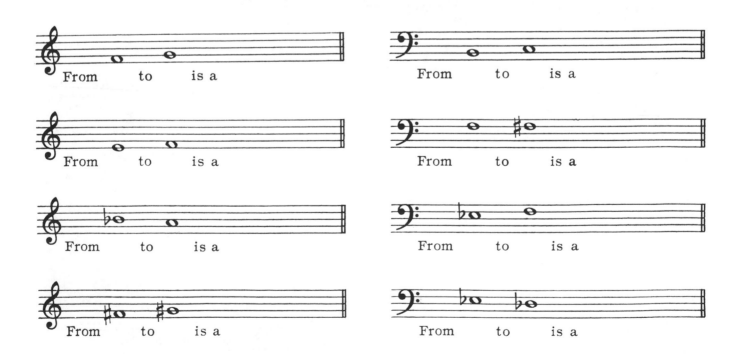

ACCIDENTALS

New hand position in C major

Shift the left hand three white keys up-ward to Middle C and practise each hand separately.

Always
Be
Careful

to observe accidentals

The SHARP (♯) and FLAT (♭) signs used to raise or lower notes one SEMI-TONE are called ACCIDENTALS.

6   THE SCISSORS GRINDER

Moderato M.M. ♩=60 - ♩.=54

mp Round and round, round and round

Goes the wheel when scis-sors are ground. The

p edge is sharp that was flat!

Scis - sors Grind - ers 'tend to that.

Play with as much expression as possible and note the new EXPRESSION SIGNS

means CRESCENDO, *a gradual increase in tone.*
means DECRESCENDO, *a gradual decrease in tone.*

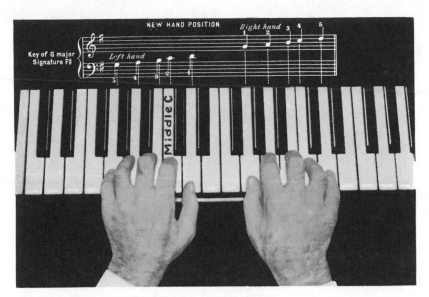

We change now to a new Key—*the Key of G major* and consequently to a NEW hand position. Note the SHARP (#) in the SIGNATURE. This means that all F's will be sharped (*played on a BLACK key*). Be sure to remember this. Place your hands in the NEW hand position and practise each hand separately before you play the piece.

7.   A SONG OF PENNY CANDY

When un - cle Ben - ny gives me a pen - ny,

I go trip - ping gai - ly to the lit - tle can - dy store.

Note to Teachers: *Pupils should be required to recite both Time Signature and Key Signature before playing each piece.*

NOTICE THE FORM of this little piece.   The entire theme is written on two **MELODY PATTERNS.**

Andante *means moderately slow*

8. THE MAN IN THE MOON

Big Moon, Bright Moon;

Sail-ing so slow-ly high up in the star-ry sky;

Big Moon, Bright Moon;

Can you see peo-ple so lit-tle as I?

TRANSPOSITION: By means of FINGER PATTERNS the pupil should now be taught to transpose the C major pieces into the key of G major and vice versa. Simply find the five-finger position for the new key and play with the same fingers as in the original key. This idea should be carried on in each new key as learned.

FOLK TUNES. Some of our most beautiful melodies came, not as you might suppose, from the pens of famous composers but from the folk-songs which have come down to us from generation to generation. These melodies originated among the people of their homeland. They were not written down but were passed along from one person to another person. Because of their charming simplicity, many of them will endure forever as masterpieces of melody. Note this beautiful old French folk-tune which consists of two very short MELODY PATTERNS.

9. THE PARTY

Old French
Nursery Tune

Andante M.M. ♩ = 60-120
Count: Three four   One two Three four

Come right in, Let's be - gin, We will have such fun to-day! Let's pre-

tend Gyp's a friend, Come to gos - sip and to play, Dogs and

toys, Songs and noise, These have made the hours fly. "Bow-wow-

wow," That is how Gyp is bid - ding us, "Good-bye."

MELODIES BEGINNING ON THE VARIOUS BEATS OF THE BAR

Melodies do not ALWAYS begin on the FIRST beat of the bar. This piece, for instance, begins *on the third beat*, adding an entirely new 'swing' to the rhythm. To produce this effect we must be careful to apply the ACCENT where it belongs—on the FIRST beat.

Count therefore: | **Three four** | **ONE,** two, THREE, four | **ONE,** two, THREE, four | etc.

The Phrasing Attack

PHRASING in music is like BREATHING in speech—we take *short breaths* and *long breaths*. If we keep in mind to make our playing of music BREATHE AT THE END OF EACH PHRASE, it will strengthen the rhythm and add immensely to the interpretation.

In playing TWO-NOTE PHRASES think of the words, DROP-ROLL and the effect will come naturally. In the following example, play the *first* note with a gentle DROP of the arm and the *second* note with a ROLL of the arm and hand in an inward and upward motion, *using no finger action* and *releasing the note* on the upward roll.

The following illustration shows the **proper** position of hand and arm as each phrase is released. The WRIST must be completely relaxed.

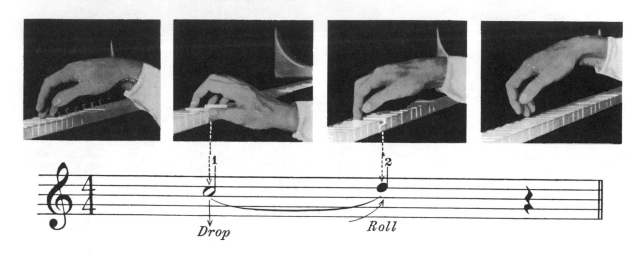

Play the following with the RIGHT hand

Play the following with the LEFT hand

The SIGN of the phrase is the curved line, ⌣. All notes under this line, except the last one, should be played LEGATO. The last note must always be played with a rolling motion of the arm *forward* and *upward*.

At this stage of progress "The HANON Studies" by John Thompson should be assigned as supplementary work. This book is issued with attractive titles and illustrations, and is especially adapted for FIRST GRADE use to develop the PHRASING ATTACK as well as all the fundamental touches used in the pages of this book.

W. M. Co. 5640

Combining HAND POSITIONS already learned

To play this piece we COMBINE the hand positions learned in Nos. 1 and 7. The right hand plays the FIVE-FINGER position beginning on C while the left hand plays the FIVE-FINGER position beginning on G.

Right hand position

Left hand position

Practise with the hands in this position then play "THE ROBIN."

10. THE ROBIN

Be sure to phrase the right hand as indicated by the curved lines using the DROP, ROLL attack.
COUNT: three | **ONE** two three | **ONE** two three | etc.,

42979

FINGER PATTERNS

Have you not noticed how easy it is to transpose from ONE key to ANOTHER by means of the FIVE FINGER pattern. A knowledge of finger patterns is also very helpful when playing *beyond* the five-finger position.

Left hand

Drop Roll

In playing THE MERRY CLOWN the left hand goes out of the five-finger position, but observe how easily the left hand trips DOWN the keyboard on a simple little "ONE-TWO" finger pattern as follows:

The right hand HARMONY pattern is also extremely simple consisting as it does of but TWO SMALL CHORDS.

Right hand

Practise each PATTERN separately before playing hands together

11. THE MERRY CLOWN

M.M. ♩ = 80

"I'm fun - ny, chil - dren, as you see, So

please, laugh ver - y hard at me."

Round dots (•) over or under notes indicate *STACCATO*—detached—short.

Be sure to observe the left hand phrasing by use of the DROP, ROLL attack.

Always

Be

Careful of the accent. The melody begins on the THIRD beat.

Count: three | ONE two three | ONE two three, etc.

Nearly every phase of life in Germany is bound together in the national tie of folk-songs—true songs of the people which reflect the moral, social and political life of the soldier, student, clerk and peasant. The early settlers in Pennsylvania and other states went to America singing these beautiful melodies while they worked. Later generations forgot the words of the "Vaterland" but not the tunes. College ditties, patriotic words, etc., have been adapted to the melodies to such effect that the songs form part of the adopted country's musical heritage.

In "THE CUCKOO," both hands employ the PHRASING ATTACK. Place your hands in the G major five-finger position and be sure you are familiar with the HARMONY

pattern in the left-hand.

12. THE CUCKOO

ff - *fortissimo* *means very loud*

German Folk-tune

EXAMINATION No. 1

1. Explain the following TIME SIGNATURES and tell where the accents fall in

   each. $\frac{2}{4}$ $\frac{3}{4}$ $\frac{4}{4}$

   . . . .

   . . . .

2. What is a SEMITONE? . . . . A WHOLE TONE? . . . .

3. Give the definitions of the following:

   MODERATO . . . .
   LEGATO . . . .
   ANDANTE . . . .
   RITARDANDO . . . .
   TEMPO . . . .

4. Write the SIGNS and meaning of the following musical terms.

   FORTE . . . . Its SIGN . . . .
   MEZZO FORTE . . . . Its SIGN . . . .
   PIANO . . . . Its SIGN . . . .
   MEZZO PIANO . . . . Its SIGN . . . .
   PIANISSIMO . . . . Its SIGN . . . .
   FORTISSIMO . . . . Its SIGN . . . .

5. What are ACCIDENTALS and what effect have they?

   . . . .

   . . . .

6. What are FOLK-TUNES?

   . . . .

   . . . .

Attach Certificate No. 1 here

Note to Teacher: *Pupils may be graded according to the preference of the individual teacher. Some teachers prefer the use of silver and gold stars; some grade by percentage, while others find the letter system of grading as used in most schools more suitable.*

When the above examination has been passed to the satisfaction of the teacher, the pupil should be awarded CERTIFICATE NO. 1 (See page 79 of this book) duly signed, dated and graded.

AVERAGE GRADE

for examination No. 1

. . . .

SCALES

THE matter of Scales and Arpeggio practice is a much debated question among piano teachers. Some teachers begin scale work quite early in the pupil's career and are very insistent in the matter of daily practice. Others look upon them as a sort of unnecessary drudgery and claim that pupils can develop just as much facility in playing the scale and arpeggio passages that occur in the books and sheet music of their repertoire. Naturally, this resolves itself into a matter of individual judgment.

THE author feels that since all music is made up of scales and arpeggio figures, or fragments thereof, pupils should be required to know something about them. All music has form and shape that should be recognized in order to aid interpretation and general musicianship. There is also a technical value to scales and arpeggio practice which cannot be summarily dismissed. Perhaps the real difficulty arises from the theory that most pupils look upon the scale as a dry, uninteresting exercise invented by the teacher as a special form of punishment. If more care were used in presenting the scale and a real effort made to have the pupil look upon the scale as a beautiful piece of musical architecture, the result would be quite different. As soon as the formation of a scale is learned, pupils should be assigned pieces in which the scale figure is employed as melody. In this way the pupil learns to greet the scale as an *interesting musical pattern*—and one which will recur many times even in elementary repertoire.

THERE are many ways to teach the scales. But most of the variations are based upon two standard approaches. Some teachers prefer the *tetrachord* approach while others find the older formula (i.e., the semitones between the third and fourth and the seventh and eighth) more acceptable. Of course, this is a matter that will vary not only with teachers but with pupils. This book has been arranged so that either approach may be made at the discretion of the teacher.

THE Finger Drills on pages 76-78 of this book contain exercises for the development of Scales and Arpeggios.

THE MAJOR SCALE

A SCALE is a succession of eight notes bearing letter-names in alphabetical order, the last note having the same letter-name as the first. The figures 1, 2, 3, 4, 5, 6, 7, 8 are called the degrees of the scale.

A MAJOR SCALE is a succession of WHOLE tones and SEMItones.
The semitones occur between 3 and 4 and between 7 and 8 as follows:

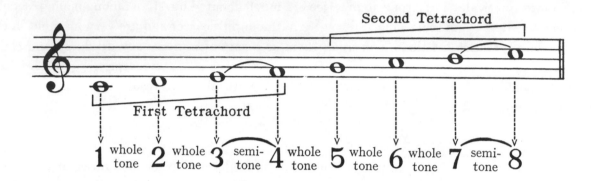

The above chart shows how a MAJOR SCALE is composed of TWO TETRACHORDS, **each** tetrachord *separated by a WHOLE tone.*
Play the scale of C MAJOR as follows, using the fingers indicated.

SCALE OF G MAJOR

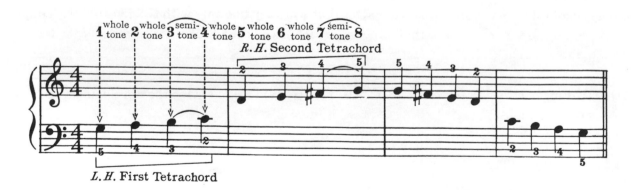

Note to Teachers: *During the progress in this book, it is advisable to adhere to the above form—the scale divided between the hands—until scale construction in all keys has been thoroughly mastered. This obviates the necessity of passing the thumb under and the hand over—a procedure which is comprehensively taken up and illustrated by examples in the SECOND GRADE book.*

SCALE OF C MAJOR—*Ascending*

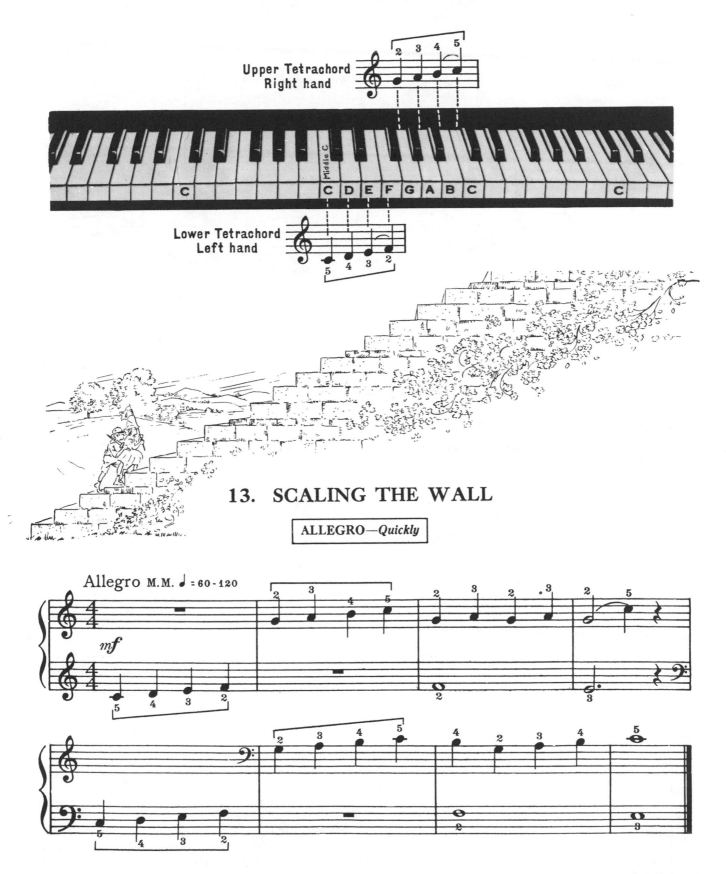

Upper Tetrachord Right hand

Lower Tetrachord Left hand

13. SCALING THE WALL

ALLEGRO—*Quickly*

Allegro M.M. ♩=60-120

Note to Teachers: *This is an excellent exercise for use in the various keys as they are learned. It should be played finally in all of the major keys.*

SCALE OF C MAJOR—*Descending*

14. THE CHIMES

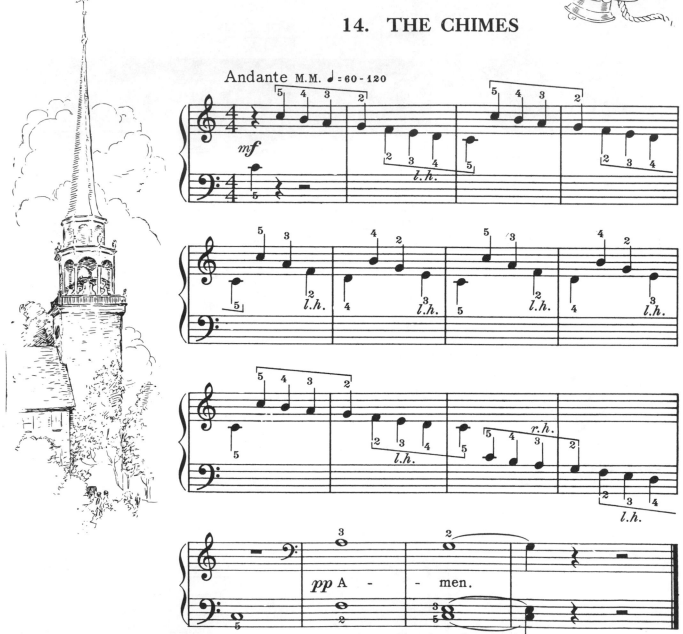

THE PEDAL

No doubt, your teacher has told you NOT to use the pedal. This has been done for an excellent reason, which you will appreciate when you have advanced a little further.

But perhaps as a reward for obedience in this matter, your teacher may, upon request, allow you to use the pedal just once in order to make THE CHIMES sound like real church chimes.

If permission is given, hold down the pedal from beginning to end. The result will be a blur which will be very unpleasant in most pieces—and that, by the way is one of the reasons your teacher does not want you to use the pedal yet. But in this particular tune, it will give a clangorous muddle, typical of Church Chimes, filling the air with overtones.

15. STEPPING STONES

Lit - tle brook, foam-ing brook, Run-ning in your bed:

Mak - ing noi - sy mu - sic at the turn a - head.

Now I cross, slip on moss, It's too late to fret!

Lit - tle brook, your step-ping stones are much too wet.

SEMITONES: The melody in the right hand of STEPPING STONES passes through 16 semitones of which 8 are *white key* SEMITONES. Can you locate all of them?

CHORD BUILDING
Intervals

An INTERVAL is the difference in pitch between 2 notes.

INTERVALS are measured by the number of LETTER NAMES contained between the LOWER and UPPER notes *inclusively*.

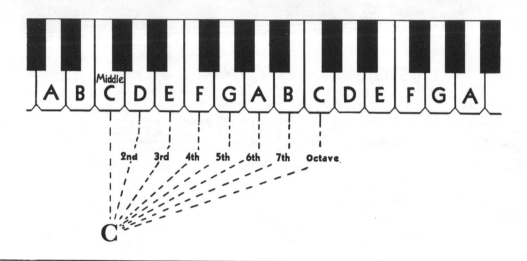

TRIADS

A CHORD is a group of THREE or more notes
All SCALES are built in steps of 2nd's. For instance : *C to D, D to E; E-F etc.*
All CHORDS are built in steps of 3rd's. " " : *C to E; E to G; G-B etc.*
The NOTE on which a CHORD is built is called the ROOT.

A TRIAD is a chord of THREE notes and contains a ROOT, a 3rd and a 5th.

EVERY CHORD IS NAMED FOR ITS ROOT

If we take the FIRST, THIRD and FIFTH notes of the Scale of C major

And sound them together thus:

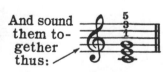

we have played the **C MAJOR TRIAD**

G is the 5th
E is the 3rd
C is the ROOT

When the C major TRIAD or any CHORD **is** played in the following manner:

it is called a BROKEN CHORD or **ARPEGGIO**.

(See Drills on pages 77-78 for Arpeggio practice)

CHORD INVERSIONS

We have learned that a TRIAD contains a ROOT,
a 3rd and a 5th. The order of these notes may
change *without changing the name of the chord.*

When the lowest note is the ROOT, the triad is in the ROOT POSITION.

When the lowest note is NOT the ROOT, the triad is said to be INVERTED.

C MAJOR TRIAD

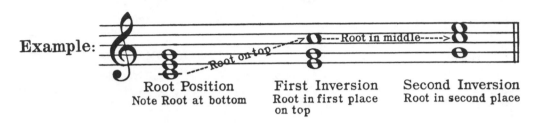

Simple rules for recognizing INVERTED CHORDS

TRIADS are in the ROOT POSITION when all the intervals of the Chord look alike; that
is, when the notes are either ALL on the LINES or ALL in the SPACES.

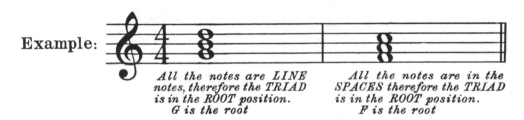

*When TRIADS are INVERTED the intervals of the chord are unlike—appear mixed; that is,
some of the notes are on the LINES and some are in SPACES.*

C MAJOR TRIAD

F MAJOR TRIAD

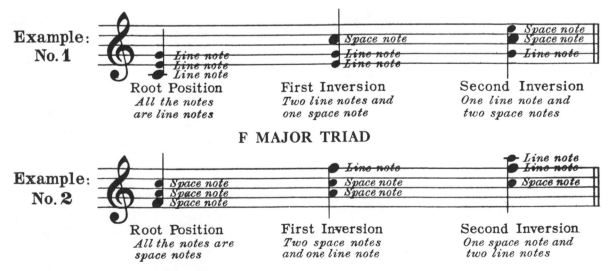

*The ROOT is always the FIRST NOTE (counting upwards) to change its position from SPACE
to LINE or from LINE to SPACE.*

C MAJOR HAND POSITION

In "MOUNTAIN CLIMBING," note how the BROKEN CHORD is used as melody. In the first two bars it is marked with a dotted circle. Locate the other broken chords and enclose each of them with a circle.

16. MOUNTAIN CLIMBING

Suggestions for supplementary solos in sheet form

FOREST DAWN in C major by John Thompson, will prove an exemplary recital piece to facilitate BROKEN CHORD playing.

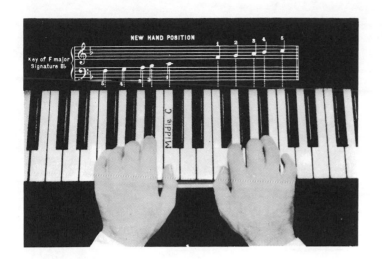

The **Key** of **F Major** has one **Flat** (♭) **B Flat.** Be sure to remember this while getting the "feel" of the keys in the new hand position and also when playing "A CHORD FROLIC."

Note how the BROKEN CHORD forms the melody. In the first bar, it is marked with a dotted circle. ·Locate all other BROKEN CHORDS and enclose them with a circle.

17. A CHORD FROLIC

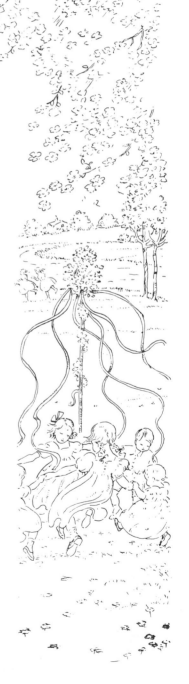

FIRST RECITAL PIECE

Here is your first real recital piece! See if you can learn it well enough to play on the next program presented by your teacher. Remember all the points you have learned thus far about *rhythm, tone colouring, expression, broken chords, etc.,* and apply your knowledge to this little piano solo.

Written Played

A WAVY LINE preceding a chord means that the notes of the chord are to be BROKEN instead of sounded together.

18. THE FAIRIES' HARP

A fairy harp hangs in the wood
Played by every breeze,
Vanished to-day are the fairy-folk
Who hung it high in the trees.

A FIRST INTRODUCTION TO QUAVERS

Note to Teachers: *Frequently, we hear differences of opinion over the question of allowing pupils to say "and" when counting quavers. As with all other controversial subjects in music, it is ridiculous to say that "This and this only is the correct way to teach." The progressive teacher applies his or her own individuality to the respective characteristic of each pupil. Whatever may prove successful with one may fail utterly with another. Experiment with ALL the approaches you know and use the one which justifies itself. It is often easier for a pupil to grasp the idea that there are TWO QUAVERS to ONE COUNT rather than "a quaver gets HALF a count." Small children know nothing about fractions. Perhaps the simplest way is to play a few QUAVERS for the pupil and allow the EAR to catch the rhythmical inflexion rather than try to appeal to the pupil's mathematical faculties at this stage.*

TWO HAND POSITIONS IN THE KEY OF C MAJOR

You have learned to change from one hand position to another in playing different pieces. Now it is necessary to make a change of position *in the same piece.* It will not be difficult, however. You have played in both positions before and you have plenty of time in which to make the shift.

19. THE WISHING STAR

German Folk-tune

See how nicely you can phrase "LIGHT-LY ROW" by using the DROP and ROLL attack on the two-note phrases. On the extended phrases DROP on the first note, connect all notes in between, and ROLL off on the last note.

20. LIGHTLY ROW

Moderato

Light-ly row! light-ly row! O'er the glass-y waves we go;

Smooth-ly glide! smooth-ly glide! On the si - lent tide.

Let the winds and wa-ters be Min-gled with our mel-o-dy;

Sing and float! sing and float! In our lit-tle boat.

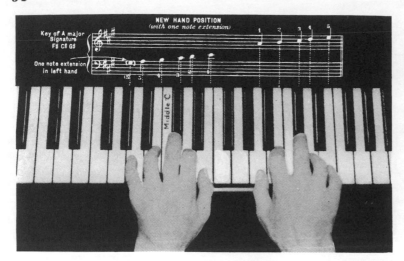

The KEY of A MAJOR has THREE SHARPS—F♯, C♯ and G♯.

Here again we have a recital piece. This calls for a smooth and beautiful singing tone.

21. LITTLE SPRING SONG

Andantino M.M. ♩=60 - ♩.=50

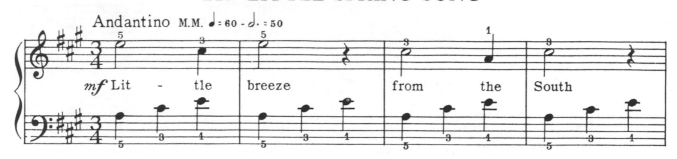

Lit - tle breeze from the South

You can sing tho' you have no mouth.

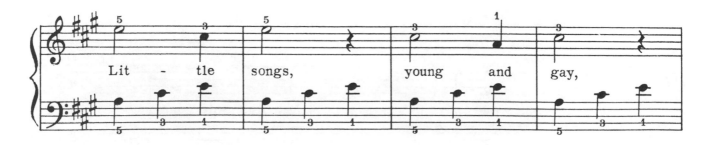

Lit - tle songs, young and gay,

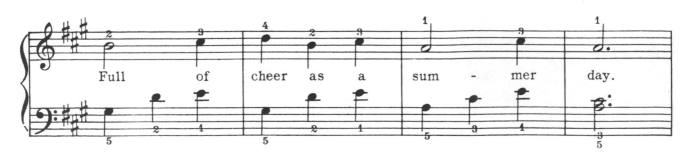

Full of cheer as a sum - mer day.

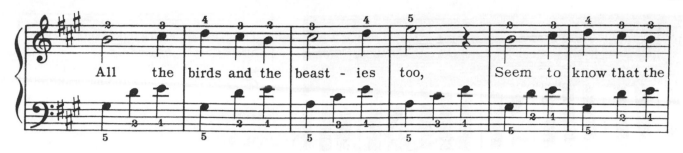

All the birds and the beast - ies too, Seem to know that the

win - ter's through! And the grass, as you pass,

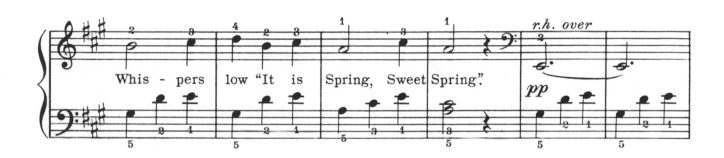

Whis - pers low "It is Spring, Sweet Spring".

r.h. over

pp

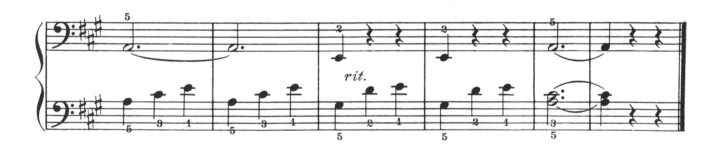

rit.

Suggestions for supplementary solos in sheet form

TSCHAIKOWSKY, MARCHE SLAV; BRAHMS, A LULLABY; two FIRST GRADE solos especially arranged by John Thompson to follow the above example showing the masters use of the scale as a melody.

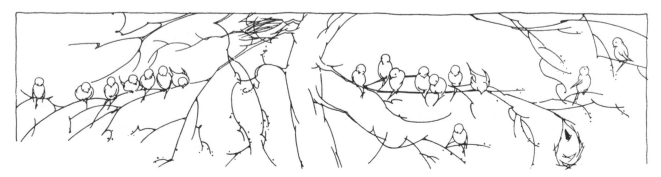

Make as much contrast as possible between the STACCATO notes and the LEGATO groups in this piece. Also see how much tonal shading you can put into it.   Note the decided shading from **ff** to **pp** in the last line.

Lay special emphasis on the notes marked with the accent sign thus,

22. FALLING LEAVES

Dry leaves float down with every gust
Because old Autumn says they must!

DANCE FORMS

In music, RHYTHM is always uppermost.   This is particularly true when playing *Dance Forms*.   It is the rhythm that gives the dance its distinctive character.   In a Dutch Dance the accent is a very heavy one. The first beat is usually phrased into the second and tossed off sharply.   Imagine Dutch Children dancing in their wooden shoes and see if you can make this piece suggest the Land of Canals, Dykes and Tulips.

23. DUTCH DANCE

A Descriptive Recital Piece

This recital piece can be easily learned if studied in the following manner:

First: Analyse the INTRODUCTION which consists of the F major chord, built up *note by note* as each new Trumpeter joins the Fanfare. ——————→

Next: Examine the left hand HARMONY PATTERN which is very simple, consisting of only two chords.

Practise them in this manner ——— *until you can make the shift easily.*

Play the left hand chords with Wrist Staccato, using a snappy, bouncing wrist. Next apply the right hand, making a nice contrast between staccato and legato. Keep the Tempo in strict March Time and play with military precision. Note the F major scale divided between the hands in bar eleven.

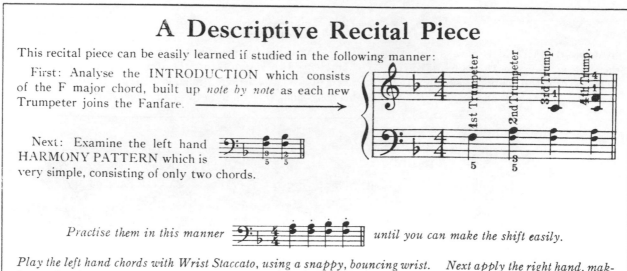

24. THE FAIRY COURT

EXAMINATION No. 2

1. Of what is the MAJOR SCALE composed?. . . . .
2. What degrees of the scale are used in building the MAJOR TRIAD?

    . . . .
3. What are INVERSIONS?. . . . .
   How many INVERSIONS has the TRIAD?. . . . .
4. What is the value of a QUAVER?. . . . .
   Grade on above ORAL examination. . . . .
5. Play the following SCALES, first reciting the KEY SIGNATURE of each.
   Grade

   C major   . . . .
   G major   . . . .
   F major   . . . .
   D major   . . . .
   B flat major   . . . .

   Average grade for SCALE playing. . . . .
6. Play the following TRIADS in ROOT position, 1st INVERSION and 2nd INVERSION, naming each position.
   Grade

   C major   . . . .
   G major   . . . .
   F major   . . . .
   D major   . . . .
   B flat major   . . . .

   Average grade for TRIAD playing. . . . .

AVERAGE GRADE

for examination No. 2

. . . .

Attach Certificate No. 2

Play this number with a "pecking" sort of wrist staccato.   The wrist should bounce freely and easily, but at the same time crisply.

25. THE TIRESOME WOODPECKER

The Woodpecker is a bird
That makes me exceedingly tired!
To go tapping like that for my food
I simply could'nt be hired!

Note to Teachers: *For further development of WRIST STACCATO use "The HANON Studies" by John Thompson, page 10.*

Practise the left hand HARMONY PATTERN before beginning the piece:

QUAVERS may be grouped together in many ways. You are already familiar with them written in this manner:

They are also written thus:

Extended hand-position for the Left hand

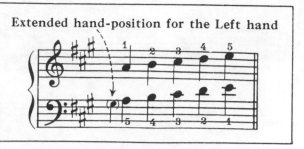

26. THE KNIGHT AND THE LADY

Riding through the green and leafy wood
Comes a lady wearing cloak and hood,
She is very sad,
Is'nt that too bad?
Surely we would help her if we could!

Lo! a gallant knight comes riding by,
How he hates to see a lady cry!
He will take her part,
Win her gentle heart,
Quietly we'll leave them, you and I.

DOTTED CROTCHETS

You have already played *dotted minims* and learned how the DOT set after a note increases the time of that note by half its value. Therefore, if a CROTCHET is equal to ONE count, a dotted crotchet will naturally be equal to ONE COUNT and A HALF,—or one full beat and half of the next one.

Introduction of the *dotted crotchet* adds a new RHYTHMICAL PATTERN to those already learned.

NEW HAND-POSITION

Practise EACH HAND SEPARATELY

By reciting the word Cumberland you will get the "feel" of the *dotted crotchet*. Before playing this piece practise this exercise and the NEW HAND POSITION.

CUM-ber-land, CUM-ber-land, CUM-ber-land.

27. "AIR" from MOZART

Mozart, as a boy

Mozart was the most musical boy that ever lived. He was born in a little town—Salzburg, in Austria, Jan. 27, 1756. At the age of four his father gave him his first music lesson; when he was 6 years old he composed a little minuet and while still a child played at court for King Francis I and Queen Maria Theresa of Austria.

44

28. A LITTLE WALTZ

This piece follows almost the exact rhythmical pattern used by Brahms in one of his most famous waltzes.

42979

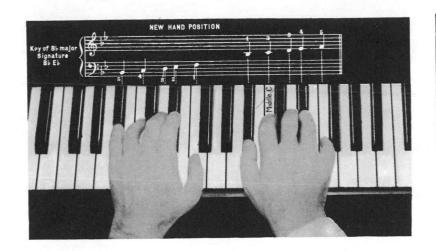

A NOCTURNE is a Night Song. It is a composition written in lyric style suggesting the peace of evening.

This one is written in the key of B♭ major. The melody in the right hand should be played with a smooth *singing tone*. Make the phrases "breathe" on the 2nd and 4th lines. Play the left hand with a light touch so that the *singing tone* will predominate in the right hand.

29. THE OWL'S QUESTION
(*Nocturne*)

Andante M.M. ♩ = 60 - 𝅗𝅥 = 58

mp When be - neath the oaks I prowl,

"Who - oo?" "Who - oo?" asks the owl.

Pleas - ant - ly I call my name,

He cries "Who - oo?" just the same.

42979

SIX-EIGHT TIME

> In six-eight time there are SIX counts to the bar and *a quaver gets one count.* There are TWO accents to the bar, the primary accent falling on the FIRST count and a secondary accent on the FOURTH count.
>
> A dotted-crotchet, of course gets THREE counts in *six-eight time.*

Note to Teachers: *When pupils can play these* six-eight *examples up to tempo they should be taught to count* two to the bar.

30. CHEER FOR THE BLUE

42979

The RHYTHM in the CUCKOO CLOCK begins on the SIXTH count.

Always
Be
Careful therefore to count as follows:

six | **ONE**, two, three, Four, five, six | etc.

Be sure to observe the TWO-NOTE phrases of the right hand, using the DROP and ROLL (Phrasing) attack.

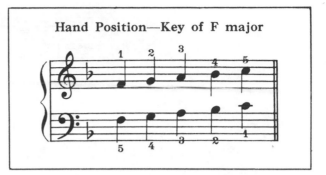

Hand Position—Key of F major

31. THE CUCKOO CLOCK

32. THE SINGING MOUSE

I'm not an ordinary mouse,
I lend distinction to a house!
Who would'nt like to see
A singing mouse like me?

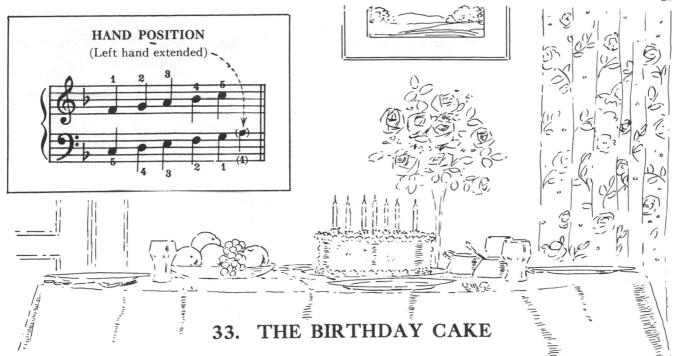

33. THE BIRTHDAY CAKE

No wonder the children to whom I come
Greet me with shouts and cheers,
I'm the glowing and beautiful Birthday Cake
That marks the passing years.

D. S. (Dal Segno) al fine means go back to the sign (𝄋) and play to Fine

PLAYING IN TWO POSITIONS

In this piece we shall play in TWO "HAND-POSITIONS."

Practise the positions separately by changing from one position to the other and back again before attempting to play "The POP-CORN MAN."

OBSERVE the STACCATO notes. It is suggested that the *wrist staccato* be used.

First Position

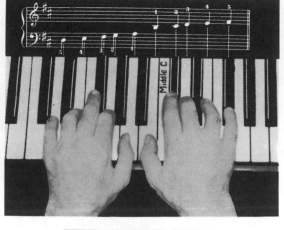

Second Position

34. THE POP-CORN MAN

D.C. (Da Capo) al *fine* means return to the beginning and play to **Fine.**

TWO "HAND-POSITIONS"

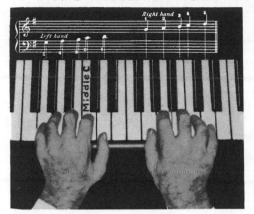

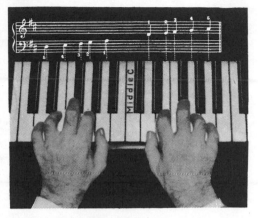

This piece requires two "HAND-POSI-TIONS" as shown here. Practise each pattern carefully.

ACCENT each note bearing this sign

First Position   **Second Position**

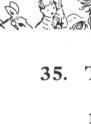

35. THE MERRY-GO-ROUND

I'm riding a Kangaroo
When I'm not changing off to a Gnu!
O, a Merry-Go-Round is fun
For every age under the sun.

SYNCOPATION

Another recital piece, this time with the atmosphere of Old Spain. *Fiesta*, the Spanish for holiday, is a time of processions, dancing, feasting and merry-making.

The TYING OVER of the LAST half of the first beat into the FIRST half of the second beat results in a RHYTHMICAL effect known as *syncopation*.   The effect will be distinguished by giving a slight emphasis to the notes marked

TO LEARN THIS PIECE; first study the HARMONY PATTERN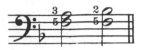

Then practise it
in this form

Now become familiar with the RHYTHMICAL pattern in the right hand.   It is practically the same

in every bar. Be sure to emphasize the notes marked

The pupil should be able to clap or tap the rhythm before attempting to play.
Follow all expression marks,
Play with good, sharp rhythm and
Earn a place on the next recital program.

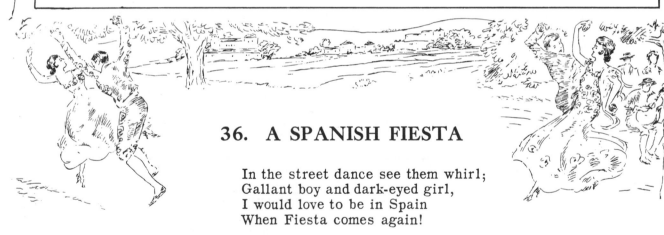

36. A SPANISH FIESTA

In the street dance see them whirl;
Gallant boy and dark-eyed girl,
I would love to be in Spain
When Fiesta comes again!

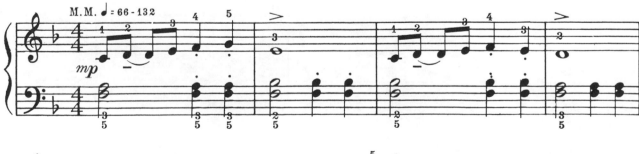

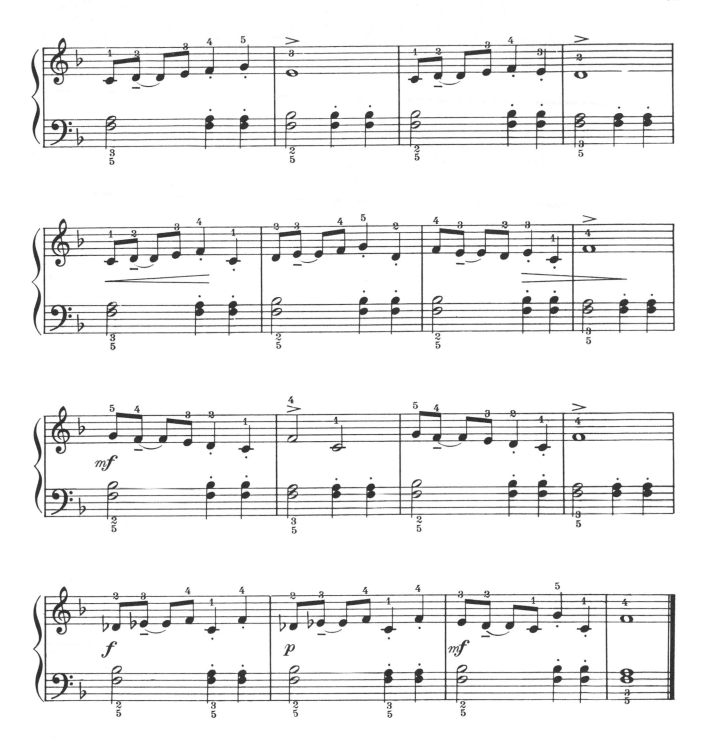

Note to Teachers: *For additional practice rhythms, see "The HANON Studies" by John Thompson, page 22.*

37. THE FOX HUNT
(*A Hunting Song*)

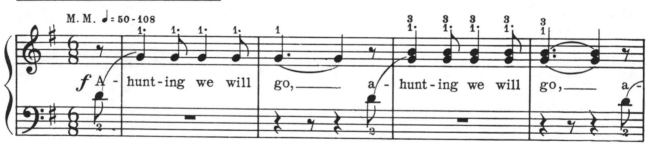

A- hunt-ing we will go,___ a- hunt-ing we will go,___ a-

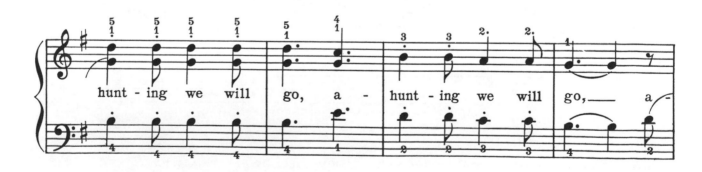

hunt - ing we will go, a - hunt - ing we will go,___ a-

hunt-ing we will go,___ a- hunt-ing we will go,___ a

hunt - ing we will go, a - hunt - ing we will go.___ Tan-

ti - vy! Tan-ti - vy! Tan - ti - vy! A - hunt - ing we will go.___ Tan-
pp

(Echo)

ti - vy! Tan-ti - vy! Tan - ti - vy! A - hunt - ing we will go.___

TWO "HAND-POSITIONS"

Two "hand-positions" in the right hand are required for this piece. Learn to play this familiar old song with feeling and it will prove a valuable addition to your repertoire.

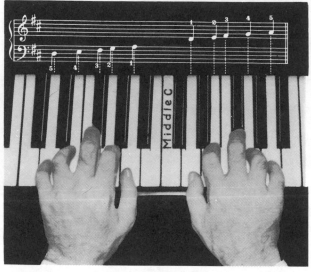
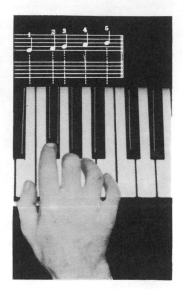

First Position   **Second Position**

38. TO CELIA

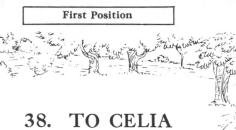
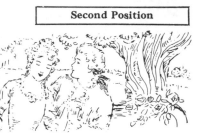

Andante M.M. ♪ = 72 - ♩. = 46

with much expression

2nd position R.H.   *1st position R.H.*

42979

EXAMINATION No. 3

1. What is the meaning of this sign, ⌢ ? . . . .

2. What is SYNCOPATION?. . . . .

3. How much extra time is given to a DOTTED NOTE?. . . . .

4. What should be uppermost when playing DANCE FORMS?. . . . .

Grade on above ORAL examination. . . . .

5. Play the following SCALES, first reciting the key SIGNATURES of each.

Grade

A major   . . . .
E flat major . . . .
E major   . . . .
A flat major . . . .

Average grade for SCALE playing. . . . .

6. Play the following TRIADS in the ROOT position, 1st INVERSION and 2nd INVERSION, naming each position.

Grade

A major   . . . .
E flat major . . . .
E major   . . . .
A flat major . . . .

Average grade for TRIAD playing. . . . .

AVERAGE GRADE

for examination No. 3

. . . .

Attach Certificate No. 3

CROSS-HAND POSITION

Second position "Old Frogs" **First position "Young Frogs"**

Before attempting this piece place your hands in the G major position (first position above) and bring your right hand over to the second position above. Practise until the movement becomes quite natural.

39. THE FROG CHORUS

Over the lily pads
Froggies at play
Join in the chorus
To greet a new day.

Young frogs sing high
And the old frogs boom low,
All join the chorus
Their good will to show.

Suggestion for supplementary solo in sheet form

THE DUTCH TWINS by Willa Ward in the Key of C major is an unusually fine recital piece to stress interpretation. It also develops cross-hand playing.

WRIST STACCATO

Use a flexible, bouncing wrist when playing this piece and see how crisp you can make the STACCATO passages.

40. THE SLEIGH

Jingle, jingle, jingle,
In our sleigh we go,
Just like old Kris Kringle
Through the ice and snow.

For pupils interested in keyboard harmony this example affords a splendid study in 2nd's and 3rd's. Find 2nd's and 3rd's and underline all 2nd's. Draw circles around 3rd's.

41. LITTLE BO-PEEP

Little Bo-Peep has lost her sheep
And looks for them sedately,
I wish she'd find them soon, because
We've had no lamb chops lately.

Suggestion for supplementary solo in sheet form

COBBLER, COBBLER a very attractive novelty in the Key of G major by Louise Christine Rebe will prove a very interesting diversion.

THE FORE-ARM ATTACK

The FORE-ARM attack is used in playing large chords. Shape the chord with the hand, allowing the fingers to rest gently on the tops of the keys. Then press forward from the elbow (*keeping the wrists loose*) and the effect will be a sustained tone of good singing quality.

HAND-POSITION
(Note *Extension in the right hand*)

HOW TO STUDY THIS PIECE

First: Learn the HARMONY patterns.
There are only FOUR CHORDS in all

After you can make the shifts easily study in this manner

42. EVENING BELLS

What say the bells
As the sun sinks down?
"Peace", they cry: "Peace
To Country and Town".

Andante M.M. ♩=60-96

Note to Teachers: *For further development of the FORE-ARM ATTACK, see "The HANON Studies" by John Thompson, page 14.*

43. PEASANT DANCE

All 'round the Maypole
Gather to-day,
Crowning a Queen
Of the beautiful May.

In "PEASANT DANCE" the left hand part represents the drone of the bass viols which were often used to make the music to which the peasants danced on the village green.

TWO "HAND-POSITIONS"
(Note Extension in left hand)

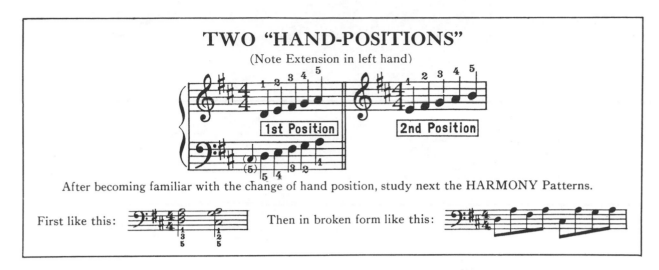

1st Position   **2nd Position**

After becoming familiar with the change of hand position, study next the HARMONY Patterns.

First like this: Then in broken form like this:

44. LONG, LONG AGO

Thomas H. Bayly

Note to Teachers: *"The HANON Studies"* by John Thompson *provide many useful examples in LEGATO and STACCATO.*

THREE "HAND-POSITIONS"

This traditional Christmas Carol requires three separate hand positions for the right hand and one position for the left hand. Practise the shift upward in all three positions to facilitate easy reading.

45. SILENT NIGHT

Franz Gruber

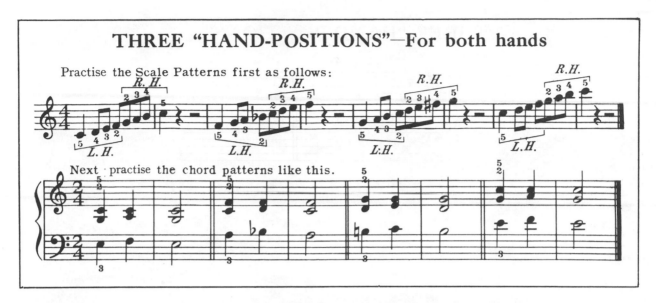

46. A KEYBOARD RECREATION

If you think you can't have fun
With Scale and Chord,
Just play this little piece!
Now, *were* you bored?

Try to interpret this characteristic piece so that the friends for whom you play will enjoy the illusion.
CAUTION: Watch the expression marks!

47. THE STREAMLINER

The train leaves the station

It gathers speed

f *The whistle blows*   f *and blows again*

p

L.H.   L.H.   L.H.   L.H.
The train begins to slow down.

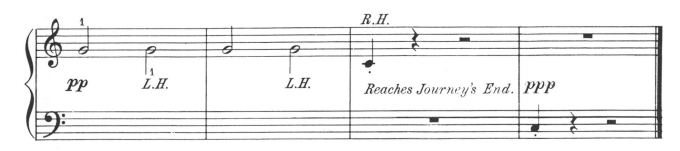

R.H.

pp   *L.H.*   *L.H.*   *Reaches Journey's End.* ppp

48. TO A SKYSCRAPER

How very strong you must be made
Not to be a bit afraid!
How can you there amid the clouds
Look down so calmly on the crowds?

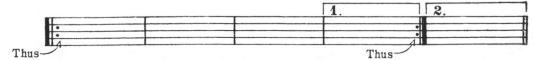

FIRST and SECOND TIME BARS: The repeat sign signifying that certain bars are to be played again

is indicated by DOTS thus:

A section to be repeated will have DOTS at BOTH ENDS:

1. **2.**

Thus   Thus

After repeating the section between the dots do NOT play the FIRST TIME BAR; instead skip to the
SECOND TIME BAR.

42979

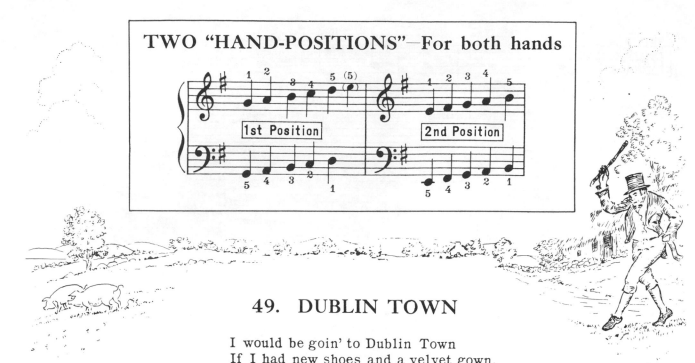

TWO "HAND-POSITIONS"—For both hands

1st Position

2nd Position

49. DUBLIN TOWN

I would be goin' to Dublin Town
If I had new shoes and a velvet gown,
But since I have neither, I drive my pigs
And fill my time gaily with songs and jigs.

Suggestions for supplementary solo in sheet form

THE BOGEY-MAN, a rhythmic humoresque in C major, 6/8 Time by Lois Long develops STACCATO and PHRASING.

SEMIQUAVERS

The TIME VALUE of semiquavers is HALF that of QUAVERS. There are TWO semiquavers

to one QUAVER and FOUR semiquavers to one CROTCHET

In this stirring piece your hands will be taken out of the FIVE FINGER position but if you observe the FINGER PATTERNS—1, 2, 3—3, 2, 1 it will be quite easy to master.

50. JOHN PEEL

D'ye ken John Peel with his coat so gay?
D'ye ken John Peel at the break of day?
D'ye ken John Peel when he's far away
With his hounds and his horn in the morning?

Folk Song

EXAMINATION No. 4

1. What is a NOCTURNE?.................................

2. Explain 6-8 RHYTHM..............................

3. What does D.C.al FINE mean?.........................

4. What is the value of a SEMIQUAVER?....................

Grade on above ORAL examination.........

5. Play the following SCALES, first reciting the KEY SIGNATURES of each.

Grade

B major   ....

F sharp major ....

D flat major ....

G flat major ....

Average grade for SCALE playing........

6. Play the following TRIADS in the ROOT position, 1st INVERSION and 2nd INVERSION, naming each position.

Grade

B major   ....

F sharp major ....

D flat major ....

G flat major ....

Average grade for TRIAD playing........

AVERAGE GRADE

for examination No. **4**

....

Attach certificate No. 4

42979

TECHNICAL DRILLS

Note to Teachers: *Appended herewith are sixteen technical exercises for the development of fingers, arms and wrists, including some drills in two-note and three-note phrasing attack. They are intended for use during the study of this book. They may be assigned purely at the option of the teacher, who will be governed, naturally, by the capacity of the pupil.*

If used, they should be taught by rote. The teacher should play each one slowly as it is assigned and allow the pupil to learn the finger and rhythmical patterns, thus making it possible to transpose into any key. These drills will do much to facilitate keyboard mastery if given a little practice daily.

First, each hand separately—then together, an octave apart.

Two-Finger Groups - The Trill

Three-Finger Groups

Four-Finger Groups

Five-Finger Groups

Two-Note Phrases
Drop - Roll

Three-Note Phrases
Drop-Connect-Roll

The Major Scale Divided between the Hands

Legato Exercise

The Major Scale with Cadence Chords

Broken Chord - Extended

42979

Broken Chord with Inversions

Root Position   1st Inversion   2nd Inversion   Root Position

Broken Chord and Diatonic Figures Combined

Ascending Finger Patterns

Forearm Stroke

Wrist Staccato

Broken Chord Drill Bugle Call

42979

Certificate of Merit

This certifies that

....

has successfully passed
EXAMINATION No. 4

THE FIRST GRADE BOOK
of
**JOHN THOMPSON'S MODERN COURSE
FOR THE PIANO**

....
Teacher

Date.....................

Certificate of Merit

This certifies that

....

has successfully passed
EXAMINATION No. 3

THE FIRST GRADE BOOK
of
**JOHN THOMPSON'S MODERN COURSE
FOR THE PIANO**

....
Teacher

Date.....................

Certificate of Merit

This certifies that

....

has successfully passed
EXAMINATION No. 2

THE FIRST GRADE BOOK
of
**JOHN THOMPSON'S MODERN COURSE
FOR THE PIANO**

....
Teacher

Date.....................

Certificate of Merit

This certifies that

....

has successfully passed
EXAMINATION No. 1

THE FIRST GRADE BOOK
of
**JOHN THOMPSON'S MODERN COURSE
FOR THE PIANO**

....
Teacher

Date.....................

*Each certificate to be cut out and pasted on respective page
when earned by pupil*

42979